D1074006

THE WORLD OF NASCAR

THE STARTING LINE:
Life as a NASCAR Rookie

DeForest Area Public Library

TRADITION BOOKS®
A New Tradition in Children's Publishing™
MAPLE PLAIN, MINNESOTA

BY JAMES
BUCKLEY JR.

Published by **Tradition Books**® and distributed to the
school and library market by **The Child's World**®
P.O. Box 326
Chanhassen, MN 55317-0326
800/599-READ
http://www.childsworld.com

Photo Credits
Cover: Sports Gallery/Al Messerschmidt
AP/Wide World: 7, 8, 9, 10, 13, 14, 16, 17, 20, 21
Corbis: 6, 11
Sports Gallery: 5, 18, 23, 26, 28 (Al Messerschmidt), 25 (Brian Spurlock)

An Editorial Directions book
Editorial Directions, Inc.: E. Russell Primm, Editorial Director; Katie Marsico and Elizabeth K.
Martin, Assistant Editors; Olivia Nellums, Editorial Assistant; Susan Hindman, Copy Editor;
Susan Ashley, Proofreader; Kevin Cunningham, Fact Checker; Tim Griffin/IndexServ, Indexer;
James Buckley Jr., Photo Researcher and Selector

The Design Lab: Kathy Petelinsek, Art Director and Designer; Kari Thornborough,
Page Production

Library of Congress Cataloging-in-Publication Data
Buckley, James, 1963-
    The starting line : life as a NASCAR rookie / by James Buckley, Jr.
        p. cm. — (The world of NASCAR)
Includes index.
Summary: Looks at the ups and downs of a professional driver, Jimmie Johnson, during his
rookie year on the NASCAR Winston Cup Series racing circuit.
    ISBN 1-59187-034-8 (lib. bdg. : alk. paper)
    1. Johnson, Jimmie, 1975– —Juvenile literature. 2. Automobile racing drivers—United
States—Biography—Juvenile literature. [1. Johnson, Jimmie, 1975– 2. Automobile racing
drivers.] I. Title. II. Series.
    GV1032.J54 B83 2003
    796.72'092—dc21   2003007687

Note: Beginning with the 2004 season, the NASCAR
Winston Cup Series will be called the NASCAR Nextel
Cup Series.

Table of Contents

I N T R O D U C T I O N

The Big Leagues

Being a rookie in any sport is difficult. You're automatically the "new kid on the block." The veterans might help you a little bit, but don't expect them to help you win! There is so much to learn, from how the sport is played to what it's like to travel around the country for a year. Attention from the press is constant, and the fans' demands can be difficult to deal with.

NASCAR Winston Cup Series racing is no different. Young drivers move up from little tracks and small crowds to enormous superspeedways filled with hundreds of thousands of fans. They're in the spotlight all the time, and there is no room for error. A mistake might not only cost them a race or a career, it could cost a life.

Making it into stock car racing's "big leagues" can take

many years of practice—and sometimes a little luck. Many drivers fall short of the skills needed to make it on the biggest, fastest, loudest tracks around. Sometimes, they make it into the series only to fail in their first seasons. A special few use their rookie seasons as springboards to long and successful careers in NASCAR racing.

In this book, we'll follow one driver through a rookie season. We'll see his ups and downs, the lessons he learns, and the successes he enjoys. The rookie we chose was Jimmie Johnson, who, as you'll see, had one of the best rookie seasons ever in 2002. After all, if you're going to tell a story, why not tell one with a happy ending?

Jimmie Johnson's No. 48 car is fast becoming one of the most feared on the NASCAR Winston Cup circuit.

CHAPTER ONE

A Fast Start

Jimmie Johnson was born to race. By the age of four, he was racing minibikes on dirt tracks in his home state of California. He moved up to motorcycles a few years later. As soon as he was old enough to drive, he switched to racing trucks in off-road desert races. He was the youngest driver ever in the Mickey Thompson Series, which races trucks on tight stadium courses.

Johnson moved up to the American Speed Association (ASA) races in 1997 when he was 22. It was a key switch, because to make his Winston Cup dream

Stadium racing in trucks is an action-packed ride through the mud—often indoors!

come true, he had to drive cars on tracks. Trucks were a good start, but the road to NASCAR goes around oval tracks.

He had success in ASA racing and soon moved up to the **Busch Series.** NASCAR's "minor leagues" are a great way for young drivers to get noticed by Winston Cup teams. Johnson's hard-charging driving skills and professional attitude got him that attention. He debuted in Busch in 1999 and was there full-time in 2000 and 2001. Late in 2001, he got his first Winston Cup start as a test run. Though he finished 39th, he caught the eye of a key person: four-time Winston Cup champ Jeff Gordon.

In 2002, Gordon was planning to co-own a team with Rick Hendrick, owner of Gordon's No. 24 car. Gordon needed a young driver for their new No. 48 car and picked Johnson.

Even in the Busch Series, the perils of racing are never far away. Above, Jimmie's crew changes tires and battles a blaze in a 2000 race.

"At first it was intimidating," Johnson recalls. "I went from watching Jeff race on TV to having him as my boss and teammate. He's been a tremendous help to me this season, teaching me about Winston Cup life on and off the track. I'd be foolish if I didn't use a resource like him."

Johnson got off to a roaring start in his first full NASCAR Winston Cup season. In February, he became the first rookie ever to win the **pole position** at the famous Daytona 500. Though he finished the race 15th, it was a huge accomplishment for a young driver, especially at the fabled Daytona.

"There's something about the history here, you can just feel the electricity in the air," Johnson said after the race.

Off to a fast start in his first Daytona 500 in 2002, Jimmie captured the coveted pole position.

"Winning the pole there was definitely one of my career highlights. I hope one of these days I'll get my car into **Victory Lane** there."

He added another big highlight in late April when he notched his first Winston Cup win in the NAPA Auto Parts 500. Johnson and his pit crew showed real veteran experience with their moves during the race. With 17 laps left, Jimmie's **crew chief** Chad Knaus called for a "gas 'n' go" pit stop. Johnson would only get fuel and try to finish the race on the same tires.

Jimmie is in the lead at the NAPA Auto Parts 500 in 2002. He went on to win the race, his first in Winston Cup.

He roared home under the checkered flag. In the stands at the California Speedway east of Los Angeles were dozens of family members and friends cheering him on.

"To do this in Winston Cup has always been a dream of mine," the excited winner told reporters after the race. "I can't believe it actually happened here, in front of all my family and friends up there in the grandstands. Thank you, California!"

Said Gordon after the race, "I knew he had a lot of talent, but I never knew the team and Jimmie would come together so quickly." The next day Johnson made an important discovery. Once was not enough. "I woke up the next morning hungrier for more wins," he said. "Winning just makes you want to win more."

Home sweet home: Dozens of Jimmie's friends and neighbors were at California Speedway to watch him win.

DIRT DRIVIN'

Jimmie Johnson got his start in off-road racing. In these races, drivers speed along rutted, dirt tracks. They follow a specific path, but it can be up the side of a hill or over a series of deep ditches. The ride is bouncy, and the vehicles use heavy-duty shock absorbers.

Many of the races are held in the desert or in scrubland away from populated areas. But fans travel many miles to watch these teeth-rattling, seatbelt-straining battles. Drivers use cars, trucks, and motorcycles specially modified to handle the harsh conditions.

Johnson remembers his time in the dirt fondly. "When you're traveling down some of these roads and you know where the big hills are, you get a 100-miles (160-kilometers) per-hour run at a big jump! That was one of the neat things about desert racing—you could do some really extreme stuff, jumping from hill to hill [in your truck]. There's really something about the challenge of trying to control a race car over extremely rough terrain."

Driving or flying? Big jumps over desert bumps are a big part of off-road racing.

C H A P T E R   T W O

Hard Lessons

Jimmie Johnson showed with his win in California that he had the right stuff to be a NASCAR driver— behind the wheel, that is. He was quickly learning that there was more to his new job than just sitting down and driving fast. In a question-and-answer session with fans on NASCAR.com, Johnson reflected on his new life:

"There are a lot of things outside the car that change. Inside the car, that's the part you look forward to and have grown up dreaming about. Outside the car, you have no clue what's coming. There are a lot of responsibilities to your sponsor [Lowe's Home Improvement Stores], your team, your fans, the media. There are a lot of things going on that eat up your time. I find myself extremely busy. I've got to climb into the car five minutes before the race and remind myself: All right, you're in the race car, this is the job, [focus] your mind.

"It's been busy, but I'm racing against my heroes and doing something I've dreamed of since I was a kid. That's pretty cool."

Jimmie pleases fans and his sponsor, Lowe's, by signing autographs and meeting with the public.

Jimmie's crew works feverishly on pit row. While
Jimmie was learning the ropes of NASCAR, his
crew was learning along with him.

He also talked about the biggest adjustments he had to make in how he raced. Winston Cup races are as much as 300 miles (483 km) longer than Busch races. The longer races meant learning a new way to race. "Not because it's physically harder for me to deal with," Johnson said, "but because I need to be in a different mindset. Here you need to be more patient. In Busch, I didn't have too much time to wait and had to force the issue sooner. Here I'm just trying to keep my head about me and keep my No. 48 in front at the end."

Though he had a win under his belt, Johnson was far from an expert. A series of mistakes became a series of lessons learned. At Richmond, he spun out late in the race while in second place. At the Coca-Cola 600 in May, he was near the lead when he overshot his pit area. Each driver has a small area in which he must stop his car in order to pit. Johnson rolled his car past his area's boundary line, and the delay in pushing it back into his spot cost valuable time. "I can't blame it on anyone but myself," a disappointed Johnson said after the race.

"You're a hero one lap and on another you're a zero."

Later, he said, "I've had plenty of reminders that I'm a rookie. I'd trade some youth for some experience in a heartbeat."

At Bristol in August, the pressure he was under started to show. He was bumped by Robby Gordon (no relation to Jeff) and knocked out of the race. As Gordon went around the track again, Johnson yelled at him and made a rude gesture to him. "If I could take that back, I would," Johnson said later.

This wreck knocked Jimmie out of the race in Bristol in 2002. It also made him lose his temper in a very public way.

"I don't need to be out there acting the way I did, and I'm ashamed it happened. But with so much on the line, contending for the championship, my emotions got the best of me. I'm a professional and need to act like a professional."

Jeff Gordon, his boss and fellow driver, understood Johnson's anger, but he hoped the rookie could use it in a better way. "He's intense, for sure," Gordon said. "You want a guy with intensity [on your team]. You just have to know when to use it." Just one more lesson every rookie has to learn, even one as good as Jimmie Johnson.

Good boss to have: Four-time NASCAR champion Jeff Gordon gives Jimmie one of the best mentors in the business.

GOOD BOSS

If you're going to have a boss, pick a good one. In Jeff Gordon, Jimmie Johnson has one of the best drivers on the planet as his boss. Gordon has won four Winston Cup season championships (1995, 1997, 1998, and 2001). In only 11 seasons, he has won 61 races and been in the top five another 101 times!

Gordon's rookie year wasn't as good as his employee's was, however. Gordon debuted in 1993, but won only one pole and no races. His first victory didn't come until his second full season in 1994 at the Coca-Cola 600. Of course, by 1995, he was the series champion, so Johnson still has a way to go to catch the boss.

In 2002, Gordon taught Johnson one final lesson as the season ended. By finishing ahead of Johnson in the season's final race, Gordon inched in front of him in the points contest. Both racers won three races, but Gordon finished seven points ahead of Johnson overall, 4607 to 4600. Look for Gordon to try to keep his employee in his rear-view mirror for a few more seasons!

Jeff Gordon wants Jimmie to do well, but not better than Jeff!

CHAPTER THREE

Rookie Milestones

Jimmie Johnson had made some mistakes, but he had learned from them. He showed just how good a student he was the week after his pit-stop mistake by earning his second victory of the season. It came at Dover, Delaware, in the MBNA Platinum 400. The victory over Bill Elliott shot him into second place in the overall standings. He would remain among the top five for the rest of the season.

He continued racking up season points over the next two months. On September 22, he returned to Dover with the rest of the Winston Cup drivers for the MBNA All-American Heroes 400. Johnson must love racing in Delaware because he became the first rookie to win both races there in one season. He also matched the record of NASCAR legend Richard Petty, who won his first two career races at the Dover track. Johnson's third

victory of the season tied an all-time rookie mark set in 1999

by Tony Stewart.

Teamwork was again the key to victory. One of the first

things NASCAR rookies learn is that it takes more than just

a driver to make a car a champion.

No. 48 is number one again in Dover. Jimmie waves
from the window as the checkered flag drops.

In that second Dover race, Johnson and his crew decided to skip taking a pit stop when the rest of the field came in during a **caution period.** Johnson jumped into the lead when racers restarted and held off veteran Elliott by less than half a second. "These races are won by teamwork," Johnson said. "My crew won the race for me today. The top four cars were all equal. It all came down to our last pit stop. They got us out first, and I was able to hang on.

"We need to make the most of this [win]," he said. "We led the most laps and won the race. Hopefully, we can break away a little bit, secure a top-five finish in the points."

Even as he was winning his third race, Johnson the rookie was still learning. With the lead in the race, he remembered something he had learned from other races. "Earlier this year, I wore out the tires trying to get a big lead on people," he said. "I've learned to look in the mirror and keep the distance the same so I can save something for the end."

Now he had a new record to shoot for. He wanted to become the first rookie in NASCAR history to lead the Winston Cup points standings. With a 10th-place finish in the Protection 400 in Kansas on September 29, he did just that. It was a huge milestone. The kid from the California dirt tracks had climbed to the top of the Winston Cup mountain.

Unfortunately, he fell right off again. At the EA Sports 400 the next week, he won the pole but finished the race 37th. Just like that, his ride at the top was over.

By the time of October's race in Martinsville, Jimmie's drive to the top had slowed to a crawl.

REMEMBERING A FRIEND

One of the sad parts of stock car racing is that sometimes drivers are killed in accidents. In 2001, a good friend and fellow driver died in a crash. Blaise Alexander wrecked his car in an **ARCA Series** race at Lowe's Motor Speedway.

On the front of Jimmie Johnson's car, there is a flame sticker on the driver's side. "That way, every time I cross the finish line, he'll always finish ahead of me," Johnson told writer Marty Smith on NASCAR.com.

Johnson and Alexander became friends as young drivers coming up in the ranks. Johnson had to race the day after Alexander's accident, and he had to "put up a mental wall" to deal with it.

"Some days or weeks I think about him a lot more than others. Sometimes you just feel him there. When you lose someone that close to you, it's a big reality check.

"But he would be loving every minute [of our success] this season."

Look closely at the words directly above Jimmie's front left tire. In the center is a yellow sticker of a lit candle. It honors Jimmie's friend Blaise Alexander.

23

C H A P T E R   F O U R

Finishing Strong

As the end of his amazing rookie season came into view, Jimmie Johnson realized just how lucky he and his team had been so far. Learning to deal with success was just another lesson.

"I'd think I'd be crazy if I thought [at the beginning of the season] that we had a shot to win the championship," he said. "We started with some realistic goals. Make races and try to finish in the top 15. Now it looks like if we pick up 20 points a race, we could be champions."

He entered the NAPA 500 in late October in second place, just 82 points behind Tony Stewart. A good result would give him a shot at catching the veteran star. But Johnson did not run his best race. On lap 139, his car slid up the track and clipped the wall. He spun out, but got control and stayed in

the race. He spun again on lap 232, again saving the car, but losing valuable speed and time. He finished in 22nd place and dropped to third overall, 150 points back.

"It was a bummer [to lose the points], but we've still got a chance at finishing up the year real strong," he said afterward.

Tony Stewart was the NASCAR champion in 2002, spoiling Jimmie Johnson's unlikely bid for the title.

"We'll just have to try to run as strong as we can at every event and see how it shakes out."

It didn't shake out too well, however. Over the season's final six races, Johnson finished no better than sixth and was 15th place or worse three times. It was a quiet ending to a terrific season. He then learned the bad news that he was not

As his rookie year ended, Jimmie Johnson had proved that he'd be comfortable in a NASCAR driver's seat.

named Rookie of the Year. Ryan Newman took that honor, even though Johnson finished ahead of Newman in the standings (see box on page 28).

In the quiet months before the next Daytona 500 signaled the start of a new season, Johnson would have more learning to do. How to make adjustments in his driving. How to help Hendrick Motorsports create a better racing car. He would also have to keep in shape and recover from the long racing season. Like many drivers, Johnson works out often to stay in top shape. He also likes to go mountain biking to help his heart and body. "It might sound funny," he says, "but you get a real workout racing cars. You use a lot of muscle groups, and it's a real workout for your heart and lungs battling the **G-forces** and turning the car."

From now on, Johnson is no longer a rookie. Some other kid will be on his tail the next year, trying to knock him off. Making the climb to Winston Cup was long and hard. Now Jimmie Johnson will learn that staying at the top of the mountain is even harder.

ANOTHER SUPER ROOKIE

As good as Jimmie Johnson's season was, he was not named the 2002 NASCAR Rookie of the Year. That honor went to Ryan Newman, who set a rookie record by winning six poles in the season. Though he finished seven points behind Johnson and only had one win, Newman won the award based on his overall performance, according to the vote of an awards committee. He tied veteran Mark Martin with 22 top-10 finishes.

Like Johnson, Newman had a lot of success quickly. He joined the Winston Cup series after several good years in the Busch Series. He also completed his college degree in engineering at Purdue University in between trips around the track.

In 2002, he started off slowly but got hot in the summer. Starting with the Tropicana 400 at Chicago in July, Newman finished in the top five in eight of 10 races. He capped that string with his first win, which came in the New Hampshire 300. He added to his points totals by claiming poles in three of the final five races.

Newman and Johnson should be among the Winston Cup leaders for years to come—from rookies to regulars.

Fellow 2002 rookie Ryan Newman figures to be one of Jimmie's top rivals in the years ahead.

JIMMIE JOHNSON'S ROOKIE YEAR: 2002

February 1   First rookie ever to win pole at Daytona 500, finishes race in 15th place

April 28   Wins first Winston Cup race, the NAPA Auto Parts 500 at California Speedway

June 2   Wins MBNA Platinum 400 at Dover (Delaware) Speedway

August 4   Worst finish of the season, 37th at the Brickyard 400 at Indianapolis Motor Speedway

August 27   Loses temper after being bumped out of race by Robby Gordon at Bristol (Tennessee) Motor Speedway

September 22   Wins third race of the season, tying Tony Stewart's rookie record; the race is the MBNA All-American Heroes 400 and is his second victory at Dover, a rookie first

September 29   Following 10th place finish in Protection 400, becomes first rookie to take the lead in the Winston Cup points standings

October 30   Falls to third in points after spinning out twice in the NAPA 500

November 17   With an eighth-place finish in the Ford 400 at Homestead (Florida), finishes his rookie season in fifth place overall, joining Ryan Newman as the only rookies in the top 10

GLOSSARY

ARCA Series—the American Race Car Association, a lower level of oval-track racing

Busch Series—a stepping-stone to NASCAR's Winston Cup Series that began in 1982; races usually are held on Saturday in conjunction with Winston Cup races

caution period—when an accident occurs during a race, a yellow flag signals all drivers to slow to the same speed; no passing is allowed until the course is safe and the green flag restarts the race

crew chief—the "coach" of the race team and the person responsible for keeping things running smoothly before and during a race

G-forces—gravity force, which increases at higher speeds and makes driving more difficult since the momentum of a car moving at a high speed pushes a driver into his seat

NASCAR Winston Cup Series—the highest level of racing in NASCAR, which stands for the National Association for Stock Car Automobile Racing, created by Bill France Sr. in 1947

pole position—the fastest driver in qualifying trials starts the race at this best position, which is the inside spot on the front row

shock absorbers—tubelike devices attached to all four wheels to help cars absorb the bounces of a roadway

Victory Lane—a special area located in the infield of a racetrack where the entire race team and family members celebrate a victory

FOR MORE INFORMATION ABOUT NASCAR RACING

Books

Johnstone, Michael. *NASCAR: The Need for Speed.* Minneapolis: Lerner, 2002.

McGuire, Ann. *The History of NASCAR.* Broomall, Pa.: Chelsea House, 1999.

Mooney, Loren. *Kids' Guide to NASCAR.* New York: Sports Illustrated for Kids, 1999.

Woods, Bob. *Hot Wheels: The Newest Stock Car Stars.* Excelsior, Minn.: Tradition Books, 2002.

Web Sites

Jimmie Johnson's Official Site
http://www.jimmiejohnson.com
To keep track of how Jimmie Johnson does in future seasons on his official site, which includes photos of him riding motorcycles as a toddler

The Official Web Site of NASCAR
http://www.nascar.com
For an overview of each season of NASCAR, as well as the history of the sport, statistics, and a dictionary of racing terms

Sporting News NASCAR section
http://www.sportingnews.com
To learn more from another leading provider of NASCAR information

INDEX

ABOUT THE AUTHOR

James Buckley Jr. has written more than 35 sports books for young readers on baseball, football, soccer, hockey, the Olympics, and more. He previously worked for *Sports Illustrated* and NFL Publishing. His other stock car books include *Life in the Pits: Twenty Seconds That Make the Difference*. He lives in Santa Barbara, California.